DALLAS DHU DISTILLERY

Text by John R. Hume

Drawings and Linocuts by Willie Rodger

Designed by HMSO Graphic Design, Edinburgh

Principal photography by David Henrie

ACKNOWLEDGEMENTS

The author is most grateful to all those who helped in the preparation of this guide-book, especially the staff of Scottish Malt Distillers, and to Miss Fiona Stewart. The historical illustrations are from the author's collection.

Historic Buildings and Monuments
Scottish Development Department

Edinburgh
Her Majesty's Stationery Office

INTRODUCTION

Scotch malt whisky is the lineal descendant of a tradition of distilling going back more than 500 years. The first people to distil spirit from fermented liquor were the Arabs; the word alcohol is derived from the Arabic *alkohl*. The reviving properties of the product were recognised immediately and it was as *aqua vitae* – the water of life – that spirit was introduced into Christian Europe. It is believed that the distilling of alcohol was introduced into Ireland in the 13th century and that it spread from there to Scotland during the 14th century. The earliest definite reference to *aqua vitae* in this country dates from 1404.

A still with worm and worm tub, from an engraving made in 1551. This is the first known illustration of this apparatus, which is clearly the ancestor of the stills and worms at Dallas Dhu.

Then, as now, the raw material was malted barley. The product, however, was different. Herbs and spices were used in the preparation of *aqua vitae*, making it more like a modern gin or other flavoured spirit. These flavourings made what was otherwise a raw spirit drinkable. In Scandinavia, Poland and Holland similar beverages are still popular. Just why the flavouring was abandoned in Scotland is far from clear, but by about 1750 "plain malt spirits" were being widely drunk. Perhaps it was simply that flavourings were difficult and expensive to get in rural areas and that drying malt over peat produced a spirit with a smoky taste, itself appealing.

In the 18th century the distilling trade in Scotland had a very chequered existence. As a major user of barley it was subject to government control and with a small number of licensed distilleries it was a manageable source of excise revenue. For these reasons in times of war or harvest failure legal distilling was not profitable. In the 1770s the industry split into two sectors: large-scale producers of spirit for the London market; and smaller-scale distillers for Scottish custom. The former concentrated on quantity and became the largest business enterprises of their day; the latter used small stills to make a smoother malt whisky.

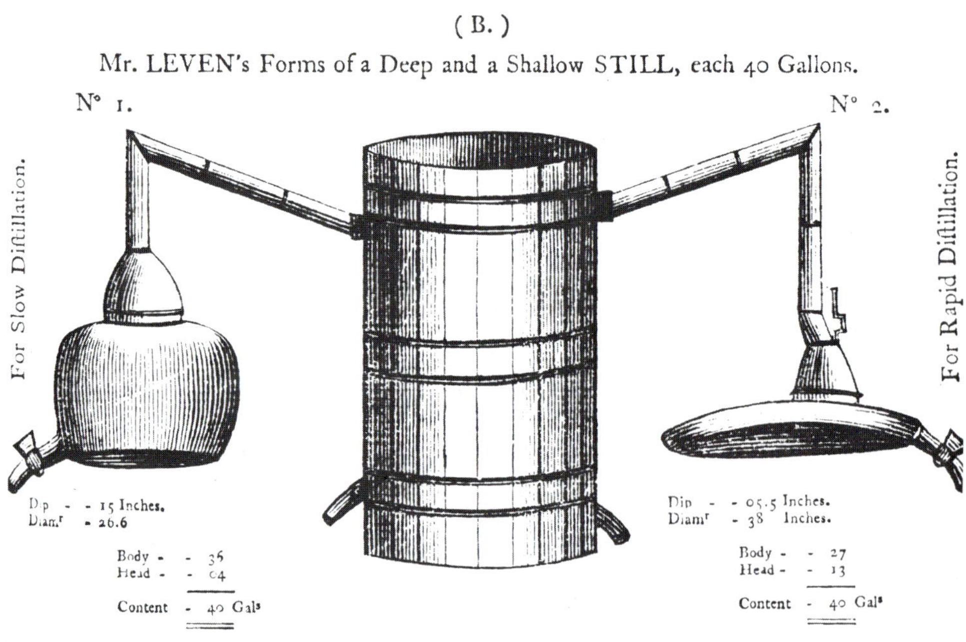

Highland (left) and Lowland stills of 1798, when duty was charged on the capacity of stills. The shallow still on the right could be worked much more rapidly than the deeper Highland still, but at the expense of quality.

This artist's sketch gives a good impression of the appearance of a small illicit distillery.

The effective prohibition of small-scale distilling during the wars which followed the French Revolution of 1789 drove the industry underground. Illicit distilling and smuggling became rife. Such practices were often condoned, and even encouraged, by landowners anxious to maximise their rent. The "Small Stills" Act of 1816 which allowed the licensing of stills with a minimum capacity of 40 gallons was only partly successful in curbing the smuggling trade and in 1823 a more liberal act was passed. Within a few years the number of licensed distilleries had rocketed from a few dozen to more than 300, most of which were in the Lowlands, or on the edges of the Highlands. Though many of these new or revived distilleries soon disappeared, the survivors form the nucleus of the Scotch whisky industry of today.

The split between the large and small-scale producers persisted and was reinforced by the invention of methods of continuous distillation in Scotland and Ireland. The Irish version, the Coffey or "patent" still, allowed spirit to be made on a vast scale, so much so that ruinous competition, based on overproduction, bedevilled this side of the trade until the formation in 1877 of the Distillers Company Limited, an amalgamation of most of the leading producers.

By that time the two sides had begun to come together. In order to reduce costs the patent still operators began using maize instead of malted barley as their principal raw material. The grain whisky produced had little flavour; on the other hand, the smoky malt whiskies of the period were often rather powerful. By mixing the two types a "blend" could be made combining the cheapness of one with the flavour of the other. This practice was pioneered in the 1850s by Andrew Usher in Edinburgh. By the 1880s blended Scotch whisky was being widely marketed overseas, especially in the British Empire, and the biggest blenders were becoming powerful.

During the 1890s the industry boomed. To satisfy ever-growing consumption – and expectations of demand – existing distilleries were rebuilt on a larger scale and new ones were constructed. Heavy, smoky malts fell out of fashion and the fruity "Speyside" whiskies came very much into favour. For that reason many of the new distilleries were built in Moray and Banffshire. Between 1894 and 1899 no fewer than 19 new distilleries were built in these two areas. Dallas Dhu is one of them.

The logic of such a massive expansion in malt whisky distilling was that blended whiskies had become popular throughout the world. Vigorous promotion of blended whiskies brought fortunes to firms like Dewars, Walkers and Haigs, and smaller operators had to compete for space in the market. To secure supplies of suitable whisky it became necessary for even modest blenders to own or control at least one malt whisky distillery. Part of the whisky from that distillery could then be exchanged for spirit from other distilleries to give the variety of whiskies necessary for a good blend.

Above: A unique illustration of a small legal distillery as licensed under the "Small Stills" Act of 1816.

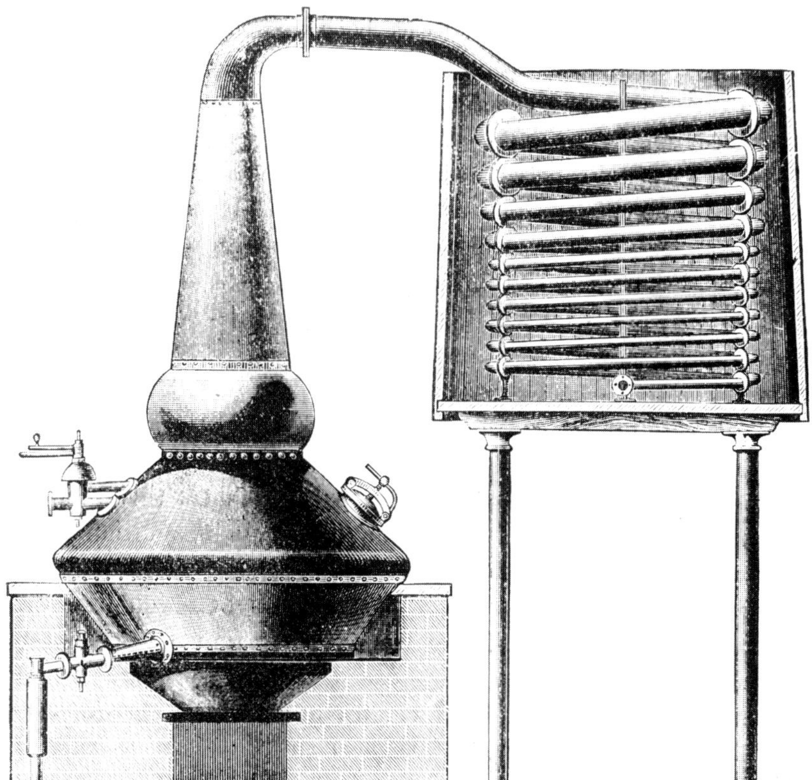

An engraving of a pot still and worm as made in the mid 19th century. The stills at Dallas Dhu are comparable in design.

A SHORT HISTORY

Dallas Dhu was one of a number of distilleries developed with the support of Alexander Edward of Sanquhar, a small estate just outside Forres in Moray. It was built on his estate for Wright & Greig Ltd, a Glasgow blending company. Wright & Greig was founded as a partnership in about 1870 to carry on business as wine, brandy and commission merchants. The firm became agents for the Auchtertool Distillery, near Kirkcaldy, in about 1876 and appear to have begun blending a few years later. Their best-known blend was "Roderick Dhu", named after one of the protagonists in Sir Walter Scott's then popular narrative poem *The Lady of the Lake*. Wright & Greig promoted the blend in colonial markets, achieving awards at exhibitions in Australia, New Zealand and India between 1881 and 1884. The firm was incorporated as a limited company in 1890, by which time they described themselves as "wholesale wine and spirit merchants and proprietors of the Roderick Dhu Old Highland Whisky". When they built a new office block in Glasgow in 1897, they incorporated a statue of Roderick Dhu in its ornate façade. Small wonder then that they included "dhu", the Gaelic word for "black", in the name of their new distillery.

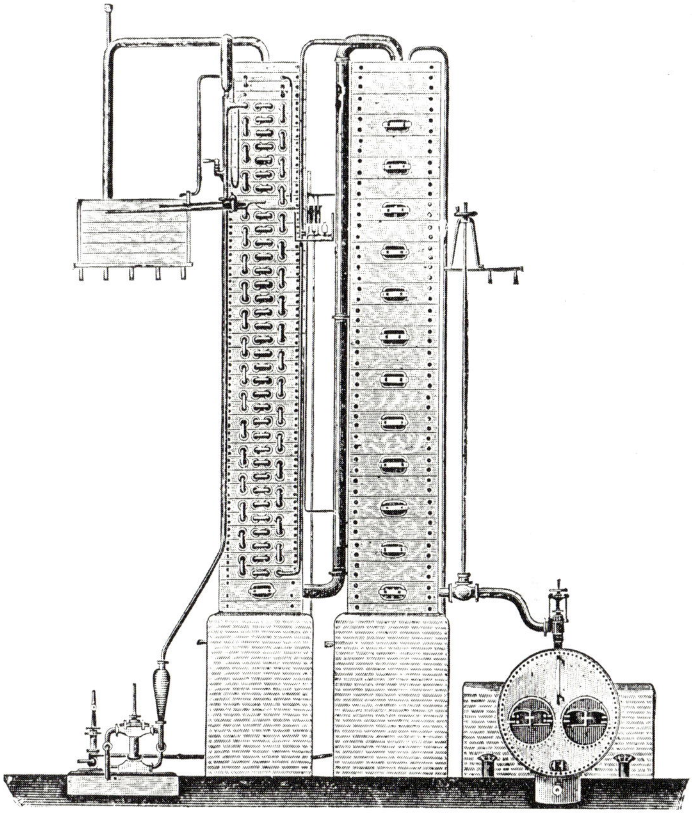

A 19th-century engraving of a Coffey still. The left-hand column stripped alcohol from the fermented wash, and the right-hand one concentrated it. Similar stills are today used in grain whisky production.

The site for Dallas Dhu was well-chosen. Water was available from the Altyre Burn and the site was close to the good barley-growing land of the Laigh of Moray. In addition, it was on the route of the Highland Railway's old main line from Forres to Aviemore, to which a connecting siding was laid. The distillery was designed by C C Doig, a local architect with a well-deserved reputation for building economical and stylish distilleries. Construction started in 1898 and the distillery was completed in the following year. The bulk of its output was taken to Glasgow for blending, but for a time at least Dallas Dhu was also sold as a single malt.

The collapse of the whisky boom of the 1890s was sudden and complete and there was no substantial recovery before the outbreak of war in 1914. Wright & Greig's capital was reduced by a third in 1910, reflecting the general lack of prosperity of the period. Prohibition of distilling during the war further eroded the position of blenders and distillers and in 1919 Wright & Greig went into voluntary liquidation. Dallas Dhu was sold to J P O'Brien Ltd, who in turn quickly sold it to Benmore Distilleries Ltd, a distilling group with two Campbeltown distilleries – Benmore and Lochhead. In 1921 Benmore Distilleries also acquired Lochindaal Distillery on Islay. Unfortunately, generally low levels of economic activity in the 1920s and, in particular, a collapse of demand for Campbeltown whiskies prevented Benmore from succeeding. Benmore Distillery closed in 1927 and Lochhead in 1928. In 1929 the Distillers Company Ltd acquired the company and dismantled the two Campbeltown distilleries and Lochindaal. Dallas Dhu was also closed and remained silent throughout the depression years of the early 1930s. It was reopened in 1936 by Scottish Malt Distillers, the malt whisky distilling subsidiary of the Distillers Company, though it continued to be licensed to Benmore Distilleries Ltd.

Fire destroyed the stillhouse in 1939, but it was soon rebuilt, only for the distillery to be closed down again during World War II. Soon after the war it helped to supply a world thirsty for Scotch whisky. Electric power was introduced in 1950. In the 1950s and 60s it escaped the expansion which characterised most older distilleries, mainly on account of its limited water supply. In 1963, however, new stills with automatic coal firing were installed and at about the same time the mashing and fermenting sections were re-equipped. In the early 1970s steam heating of the stills was installed to replace coal firing.

Demand for Scotch whisky, which had grown steadily since World War II, peaked in 1979 and in the ensuing years it became clear that there was more whisky in warehouses than was necessary to meet forecasts of demand. In 1983 the Distillers Company decided to close some of its smaller and older distilleries in order to match production more closely to demand.

Craigellachie Distillery as completed in 1891. This was one of the distilleries promoted by Alexander Edward, on whose estate at Forres Dallas Dhu was later built.

W P Lowrie & Co were the blenders of James Buchanan's Black & White whisky, and operated on a larger scale than Wright & Greig. This view of Lowrie's blending hall in the 1890s conveys the character of blending at the time when Dallas Dhu was planned.

The staff at Dallas Dhu at the time of closure in 1983.

Dallas Dhu was one of those selected for closure. Retrenchment in whisky distilling for the first time in a quarter of a century focused attention on an industry which had become one of Scotland's most important revenue earners and a part of the nation's consciousness. This led Historic Buildings and Monuments to look at all the malt whisky distilleries in Scotland to select one which might be preserved. Of all those available – and indeed of all those examined – Dallas Dhu proved to be the most complete, the most nearly original and one of the smallest. Through the generosity of Scottish Malt Distillers and its parent company the Distillers Company Ltd, Dallas Dhu was assigned to the Secretary of State for Scotland in 1986. In presenting the distillery to the public it is being maintained in the condition in which it was last used, with buildings of the 1890s and equipment of the 1960s and 70s, the high point of distilling to date. Facilities for visitors have been installed with a minimum of alteration to the fabric of the buildings.

Wright & Greig's Glasgow offices at 64 Waterloo Street, built just before Dallas Dhu. Above the door are statues of Roderick Dhu (left) and Fitzjames, the antagonists in Sir Walter Scott's narrative poem "The Lady of the Lake".

A quarter-cask (28 gallons) filled by Benmore Distilleries in 1924 and still preserved at Dallas Dhu. The cask originally held sherry.

DALLA
DIST

1. The malt barn

2. The kiln

3. The mash house

DHU
LERY

4. The tun room

5. The stillhouse

6. The warehouse

DISTILLING AT DALLAS DHU: A SHORT TOUR

Dallas Dhu is a typical small malt whisky distillery. This description of distilling therefore is intended not only to explain the process of converting barley and water into malt whisky but also as a guide to the sequence of areas in the distillery.

MALTING

At Dallas Dhu malt was made from barley in a two-storey building known as the malt barn. For most of the distillery's active life barley arrived in sacks by road or in rail wagons. The sacks were hoisted by block and tackle to the upper floor of the malt barn, known as the barley loft. Here the barley was stored in heaps until wanted for malting. From the 1960s barley came in bulk by lorry and was lifted to the barley loft by a bucket elevator. Local barley was generally used.

STEEPING

To start the process of malting, barley has to be soaked in water. This was done in the two large cast-iron tanks (steeps) at the west end of the barley loft. Barley was shovelled from the loft through holes in the floor on to a conveyor which took it through a cleaning machine, then along another conveyor in the roof of the loft and into water-filled steeps. After 48 hours the water was drained off and the wet barley was shovelled through doors in the floors of the tanks into barrows.

A figure of a maltman ploughing the sprouting barley at Dallas Dhu. The process of floor malting ceased here in 1968.

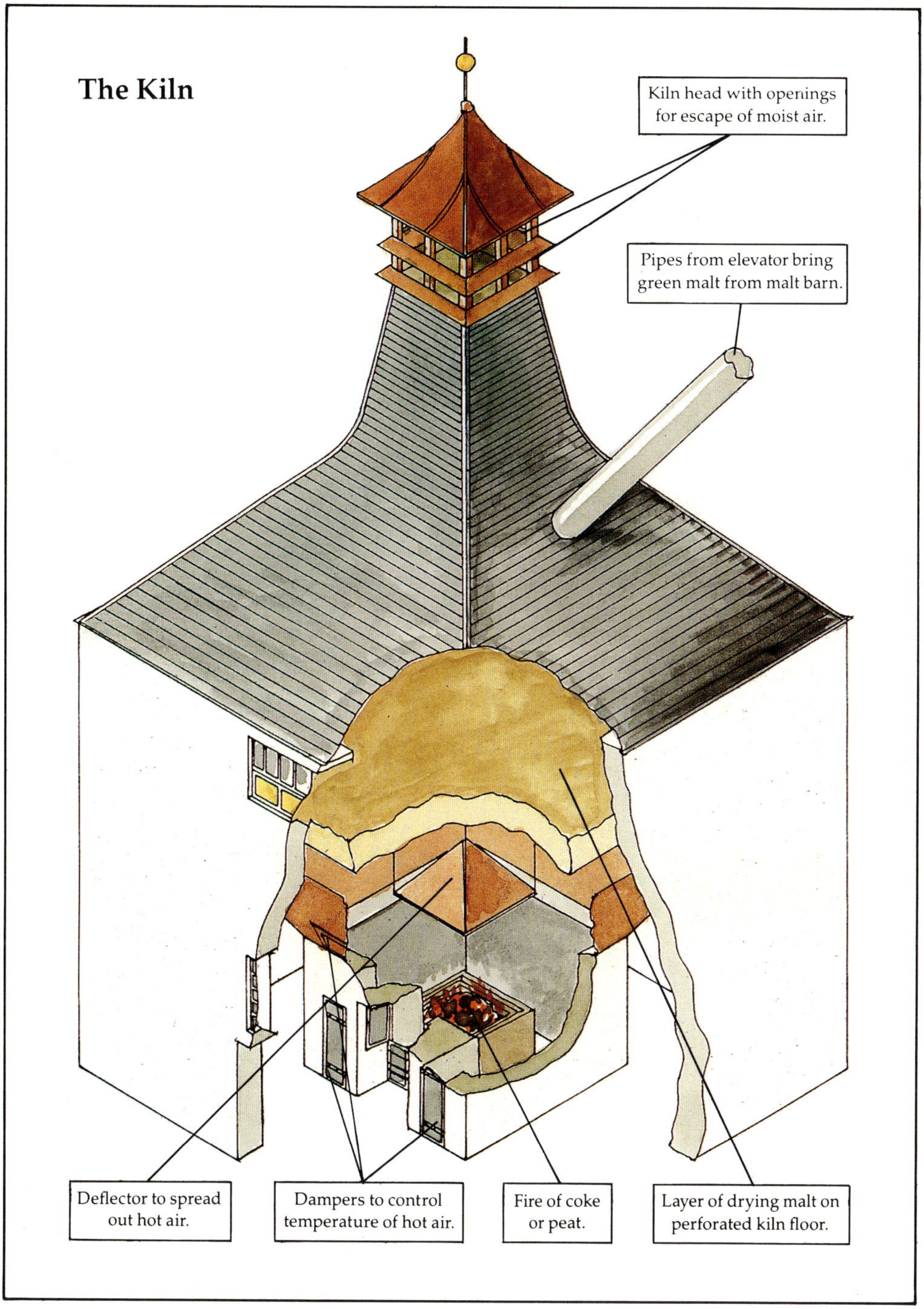

How the kiln worked. The peat or coke fire at the base warmed air which was drawn through the bed of moist malt, removing water as vapour which escaped through the kiln head.

GERMINATION

The moistening of the barley in the steeps caused the individual grains to begin to grow. The sprouting grain was then spread out, thickly at first, on the concrete malting floor. To prevent the new rootlets and shoots getting tangled and to keep the temperature of the mass right, the bed of barley was ploughed and turned regularly during this week-long stage. While this was being done, the sprouting grain was spread out over the whole of the floor. After about a week, when the shoots of the growing barley were about three-quarters the length of the grains, the grain, now known as green malt, was lifted and taken by elevator to the top of the kiln for drying. At this stage the insoluble starch in the barley grain had been split up into malt sugar and soluble starches.

DRYING

The kiln consists of a tower with a floor made of woven wire near the top. At the bottom of the tower is a fireplace with an arrangement of doors and shutters to control the temperature of the hot air generated by the fire. Hot air was drawn through the bed of moist barley by the chimney effect of the tall, pagoda-shaped kiln head. The green malt dried gradually and was turned regularly with shovels to aid even drying. Coke was used as the fuel, with peat added to give a slight smoky flavour to the malt.

Stoking the kiln fire. Peat was used at the start, when the soft, moist malt could capture the flavours in the peat smoke. Drying of the malt was completed with coke as a fuel.

STORAGE

After drying, the finished malt was shovelled into wooden bins, termed the malt deposit. Here it was allowed to "rest" for a few weeks to prepare it for mashing.

MILLING

The next stage in making malt whisky was to crush the malt to form a coarse meal, known as grist. A quantity of malt was weighed out, then fed to the malt mill, where pairs of steel rollers cracked open the grains of malt to give a mixture of husks, fragments of kernel and dust. The setting of the rollers was of great importance, as, unless the balance of the three constituents was right, the next stage of the process, mashing, would not be efficient. The mash man had to check the composition of the grist regularly. The grist from the mill was transferred to a hopper in the mash house.

MASHING

At this stage the two crucial ingredients in the making of malt whisky came together. Mashing is rather like making tea, with grist instead of tea leaves, and hot, rather than boiling water. The mashing water was heated using steam in tanks above the circular mash tun. The hot water, known as liquor, was then run into the mashing machine, a copper tube with a rotating screw inside it. Here it mixed with grist from the grist hopper and ran into the large, circular mash tun. The mixture was stirred by revolving rakes. The hot water extracted the sugar and soluble starches from the grist and the action of a natural chemical – diastase – on the starches split them up into sugars. The sweet liquid thus formed – known as worts – ran off through perforated floor plates and was pumped through a cooler into a fermenting vessel or wash back. The husks left behind still contained some sugars, so more water was added, the mixture stirred, and the resultant weak, sugary liquid added to that in the wash back. A second washing produced a very weak sugar solution that was used for the first water of the next mashing. The remaining husks – draff – were removed and sold to local farmers as cattle food.

Right: The malt mill. Within the grey casing are two pairs of steel rollers for crushing the malt. This technique has been used for more than 200 years.

Re-creation of the operation of sampling fermenting malt liquor (wash) to check the progress of fermentation.

FERMENTING

The conversion of the sugars in the sweet, brownish worts into alcohol was carried out by the action of yeast. At Dallas Dhu the yeast was brought in in block form and mixed with water in a stainless steel tub. The liquid mixture was then pumped up to the tun room and run into the newly-filled wash back. There are six wash backs at Dallas Dhu, all made of larch, with steel hoops, and each containing about 3900 gallons (17100 litres). The yeast immediately began to "work", the organisms growing and dividing with great rapidity. At the height of the fermentation the liquid became quite hot and frothed up as carbon dioxide gas was evolved. Rotating blades – switchers – cut off the head to prevent loss of liquid. After about two days fermentation was complete and the creamy brown liquid, now known as wash, was ready for distilling. At this stage it contained about 6% alcohol by volume, together with flavours carried over from the malt and produced in the wash back. By this time much of the character of the mature whisky had already been formed.

The worm tubs, in which cold water flowed through the copper spiral pipe in which the vapour from the stills condensed.

DISTILLING

This is the heart both of the making of Scotch whisky and of its mystique for it is in the distilling that the quality of whisky produced can be more readily changed than at any other stage. There are two stills at Dallas Dhu, reflecting the division of the process into two parts. The first was the concentration of the weak alcohol solution produced by fermentation. This was done in the larger, wash still, into which was run the contents of a wash back. It was heated by steam which flowed through hollow cylindrical vessels, known as kettles. These encouraged the thorough mixing of the liquid in the still. When the wash boiled, it started to froth, as it contained solid particles of yeast. The stillman then had to control the rate of heating to allow as much alcohol as possible to distil over without the mixture boiling over. The alcohol and water in the vapour were condensed into liquid by passing it through a

Below: A re-creation of the filling of the wash still, with the spirit still in the foreground.

spiral copper tube – the worm – immersed in a vat of cold water – the worm tub – situated outside the stillhouse. The liquid – low wines – ran through the spirit safe into a cast-iron tank in the receiver room. The concentration of alcohol in the low wines could be tested in the spirit safe, allowing the stillman to judge when to stop distilling. At Dallas Dhu the residue in the wash still – pot ale – was run into the Forres town sewage disposal system, but in other distilleries it is collected, concentrated, and either sold dried or incorporated with dried draff as dark grains. Both are valuable for feeding cattle.

The low wines were pumped from the receiver up to a tank above the stills – the low wines and feints charger. From this they were run into the second still, the spirit still, in which the dilute alcohol was concentrated and refined.

During fermentation, substances other than alcohol are produced by the yeast. Some of these are strongly flavoured and if too concentrated can spoil the flavour of the whisky. Fortunately, these boil either at a higher or at a lower temperature than alcohol itself and their concentration can be controlled during the second stage of distillation. The spirit still is similar to the wash still, though slightly smaller, and is heated by a coil of stainless-steel pipes rather than by kettles. Like the wash still, the spirit has a worm to condense the vapour. When the low wines come to the boil, the first part to distil off is known as the foreshots. This turns cloudy when mixed with water. The stillman made this test in the spirit safe, running the foreshots into the same tank as the low wines. When the foreshots had been distilled off, the stillman diverted the flow of liquid into an oak vat – the spirit receiver. This, the "middle cut", would become malt whisky, but at that stage it was known as "plain British spirits", or just "spirit".

When distilling of the "middle cut" is complete, the distillate again becomes cloudy when mixed with water. This portion is known as the "feints" and has a strong and characteristic odour. It, too, was run into the same receiver as the low wines. When all the useful products had been distilled off, the residue in the still, known as spent lees, was run to waste, though the heat remaining in it was used to preheat the next batch of liquid to be distilled. The newly-made spirit was not a plain mixture of alcohol and water: it contained smoky flavours from the peat used to dry the malt and some of the flavours produced during fermentation. The proportion of these carried over depended partly on the judgement of the stillman and partly on the design of the stills.

A worm in its tub. The diameter of the copper pipe reduces towards the base, making the building of a worm a fine example of the coppersmith's art.

The spirit safe, in which the produce of the stills is checked for quality without the stillman being able to tamper with it.

A re-creation of cask filling in the filling store.

Below: Sampling the contents of a cask for quality and strength before removal from the warehouse.

Below right: Examples of different sizes of cask used for maturing whisky. From the left there are a quarter cask, an American barrel, two hogsheads and two butts. The left-hand butt is a re-used sherry cask.

FILLING AND MATURING

The newly-distilled spirit was pumped from the oak receiver through to a similar but larger cask in the filling store. Here, under the supervision of a Revenue Assistant representing HM Customs and Excise, it was run into oak casks for maturing. The casks used were weighed both empty and full and the weight per unit of volume (specific gravity) of the spirit determined by a hydrometer. This allowed the volume of spirit of a standard temperature to be calculated. This quantity was stencilled on the end of the cask, together with the year of production, the name of the distillery and a serial number. These are all necessary for control of stocks during that long maturing process.

Three sizes of casks are generally used in maturing Scotch whisky: the butt, holding about 110 gallons (495 litres), the hogshead, taking about 55 gallons (250 litres), and the American barrel, containing about 42 gallons (190 litres). All casks used are second-hand, either from the United States, where they have been used to mature bourbon whisky, or from Spain, where they have held maturing sherry. The casks are charred inside, which helps in the maturing process.

Maturing takes place in the warehouses, where the casks are stored in tiers, three high. The casks are checked regularly to ensure that they are not leaking and that pilfering is not taking place. The traditional warehouse was both cool and dark, with an earth floor: there are two of these at Dallas Dhu. Spirit must be matured for a minimum of three years before it is legally Scotch whisky, but at Dallas Dhu it was frequently held for longer. During maturing, changes take place in the flavours, removing the sharpness, and some of the alcohol is lost by evaporation: this is "the angels' share"! When whisky is due to leave the warehouse, the quantity of spirit in each barrel is carefully calculated, and it is on that volume that duty must be paid.